STAGE 2

Dolphin Talk

Whistles, Clicks, and Clapping Jaws

by Wendy Pfeffer • *illustrated by* Helen K. Davie

HarperCollins*Publishers*

For Mimi,
who swam with dolphins and has befriended all creatures.
With thanks to Dr. Ann E. Bowles, senior staff biologist
at the Hibbs–Sea World Research Institute in San Diego, California,
for sharing her extensive knowledge of dolphins with me.
—W.P.

Thanks to Chris De Angelo
at the National Aquarium in Baltimore for her expert advice

Especially for Kay
—H.K.D.

The *Let's-Read-and-Find-Out Science* book series was originated by Dr. Franklyn M. Branley, Astronomer Emeritus and former Chairman of the American Museum–Hayden Planetarium, and was formerly co-edited by him and Dr. Roma Gans, Professor Emeritus of Childhood Education, Teachers College, Columbia University. Text and illustrations for each of the books in the series are checked for accuracy by an expert in the relevant field. For more information about Let's-Read-and-Find-Out Science books, write to HarperCollins Children's Books, 1350 Avenue of the Americas, New York, NY 10019, or visit our website at www.letsreadandfindout.com.

Library of Congress Cataloging-in-Publication Data
Pfeffer, Wendy.
    Dolphin talk : whistles, clicks, and clapping jaws / by Wendy Pfeffer ; illustrated by Helen K. Davie.
        p.   cm. — (Let's-read-and-find-out science. Stage 2)
    Summary: Describes how dolphins communicate with each other in squeaks, whistles, and pops.
    ISBN 0-06-028801-9 — ISBN 0-06-028802-7 (lib. bdg.) — ISBN 0-06-445210-7 (pbk.)
    1. Dolphins—Behavior—Juvenile literature.   2. Animal communication—Juvenile literature.   [1. Dolphins.
2. Animal communication.]   I. Davie, Helen, ill.   II. Title.   III. Series.
QL737.C432 P49   2003   2001039518
599.53'1594—dc21   CIP
                                                                                                              AC

Typography by Elynn Cohen   1 2 3 4 5 6 7 8 9 10   ❖   First Edition

Dolphin Talk

Dolphins swim, splash, glide, and leap gracefully over the waves in every ocean on Earth. Sailors once called the ocean a "silent world." But it's not.

The dolphin's dark underwater world is alive with sounds: crashing waves, the crackle of snapping shrimp, the songs of humpbacks, the shrieks of killer whales, and the grunts, croaks, and squeaks of a million fishes.

People use spoken sounds to let other people know who they are, where they are, and how they feel.

Dolphins use whistling sounds to let other dolphins
know who they are, where they are, and maybe even
how they feel.

Nasal cavity and air sacs

Blowhole

Melon

click click click click click click click

A dolphin makes sounds by pushing air back and forth between air sacs in the nasal cavity below its blowhole. These clicks, whistles, and squeaks move out into the water.

These dolphin sounds are made like the sounds
you make when you stretch the neck of a balloon
between your fingers and then let the air escape slowly.
Babies make gurgling sounds and squeals before they
learn to talk. Dolphin calves chirp and squeak before
they learn to whistle.

When this child gets lost, her mother looks for her. She calls her name loudly. The child recognizes her mother's voice and calls back. The mother recognizes the familiar sound and finds her child.

When a young dolphin gets lost, its mother looks for it. She may release bubbles and whistle loudly. The calf recognizes its mother's whistle and calls back. The mother recognizes the familiar call and finds her calf.

A dolphin can also find its calf, or anything else, by making clicking sounds instead of whistles.

In dark, murky waters where a dolphin cannot see, it sends clicks from its air sacs to its melon. From the melon the dolphin aims the clicks the same way a person might aim a flashlight beam. The dolphin sends out a beam of sound like the flashlight sends out a beam of light.

The sound beam hits an object and an echo bounces
back. The echo travels through the dolphin's lower jaw
to its ear, then to its brain. Now the dolphin knows
where the object is. When a sound beam and an echo
locate an object, the process is called echolocation.

400 FT.

10 FT.

Echolocation works like the sonar on a submarine,
only better. Scientists are working hard to make a sonar
that works as well as a dolphin's.

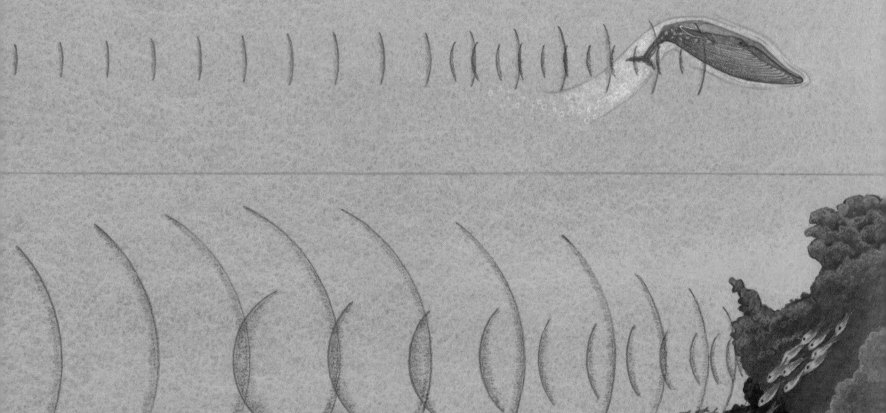

Dolphins can hear so well underwater, they can locate an object as tiny as a pea. When dolphin clicks bounce off an object, the echoes that return tell the dolphin the object's shape, as well as its size and location.

Dolphins can tell the difference between echoes bouncing off an aluminum can and those bouncing off a tin can. They can tell if a fish is dead or alive.

When this child misbehaves, her mother uses sounds called words to tell her, "Stop!"

Dolphins use movements to scold their young. When a young dolphin misbehaves, its mother may move her head up and down many times.

The young dolphin sees this movement and stops what it is doing.

When it is upset, a dolphin may make loud popping noises. It might clap its jaws, slap its tail, make a big cloud of bubbles, and even hit the water with its entire body.

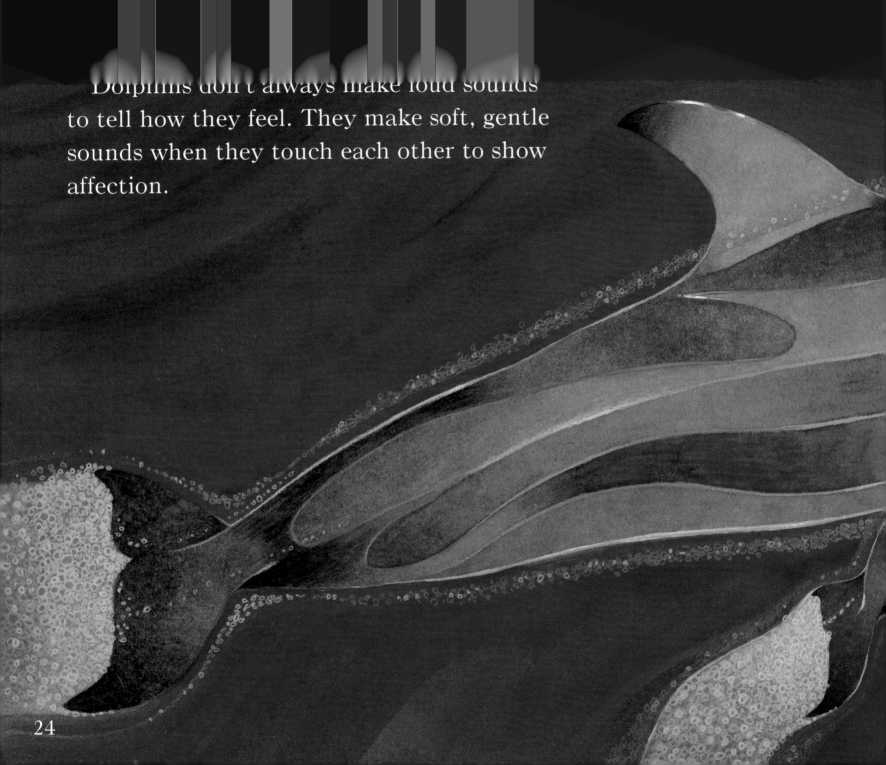

Dolphins don't always make loud sounds to tell how they feel. They make soft, gentle sounds when they touch each other to show affection.

Dolphin whistles always sound like whistles. But when a dolphin clicks faster or slower, the clicks can sound like a door creaking or a cat mewing.

Dolphins can use sounds to chirp, squeak, rattle, burp, moan, and groan.

25

Scientists think dolphins use sounds to exchange information just as people use words to exchange information.

People also communicate with one another by the way they act, how they look, how they move, and even how they whistle, click their fingers, and clap their hands.

Dolphins communicate with one another by the way they act, how they look, how they move, and how they whistle, click, and clap their jaws.

Dolphins are not the only sea creatures to communicate with sound. A stranded pilot whale whistles when in distress.

A humpback whale's song helps it to stay in contact with other whales.

A sperm whale sends out
clicks that sound like
the hoofbeats of
galloping horses.

And the shrieks of killer whales frighten the belugas.

29

The dolphin's dark underwater world is not silent. Chirps, rattles, squeaks, shrieks, burps, moans, groans, croaks, crackles, whistles, clicks, clapping jaws, slapping tails, and loud popping sounds bounce around in the water. Perhaps someday we'll be able to understand what they all mean.

31

FIND OUT MORE ABOUT DOLPHINS

New Names

At recess time, during a party, or just after school one day, tell your friends that you can whistle your own name. Then whistle the number of syllables in your name and put the accent on the right syllable. For example, Jenn'-i-fer could be three notes, the first one being the loudest. Then ask your friends to whistle a series of notes or a pattern of clicks to represent their names.

Tell each friend that the "tune" they whistled or the pattern of clicks they made is their new name. Have fun by calling your friends by their new names.

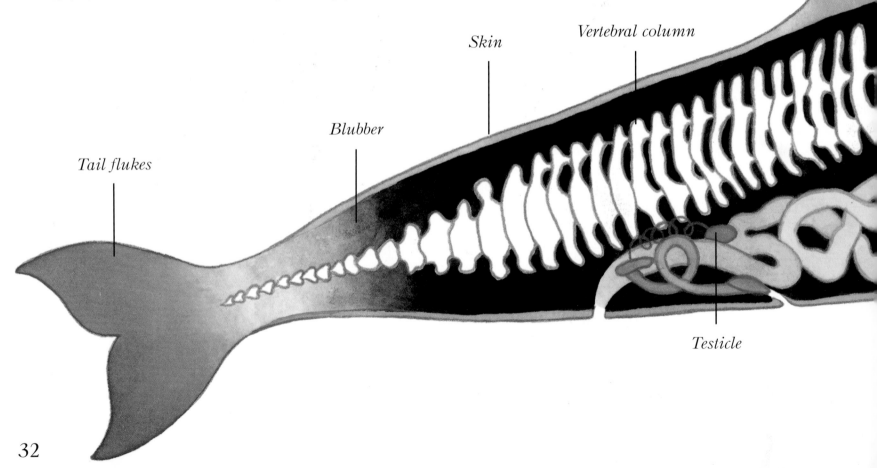

Skin

Vertebral column

Blubber

Tail flukes

Testicle

Echolocation You Can Do

Stand across from a tall wall or building. Shout "Hello" and listen to the wall or building say "Hello" right back to you. This shows how echolocation works for a dolphin. Instead of words it uses clicks. The clicks hit what is in front of the dolphin and bounce back to it.

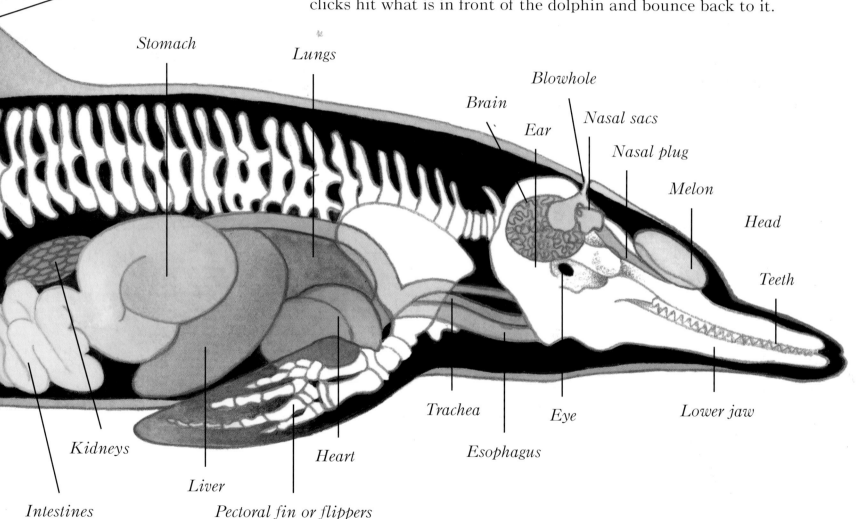

Dorsal fin

Stomach

Lungs

Brain

Blowhole

Ear

Nasal sacs

Nasal plug

Melon

Head

Teeth

Lower jaw

Eye

Trachea

Esophagus

Heart

Liver

Pectoral fin or flippers

Kidneys

Intestines